"*Charles Reddig in 2018, just prior to his 94th birthday, posing with some of his military medals, including his most prized medal- the Distinguished Flying Cross. He is also holding the cowrie shell his headhunter friend Chitabu had given to him during WWII.*

A closeup of the cowrie shell Charlie's's headhunter friend, Chitabu, in the Gilbert Islands dove in the ocean to get for him during WWII

REMEMBERING THE CLOUD
THE TRUE STORY OF WWII PILOT
CHARLIE REDDIG

As Told To His Daughter

Cover photo: from left to right: "Rossi" Rossetti, John Baldasti, Sergeant
Frist Class Charlie Reddig, Leslie Gordon Furst, and Paul Ross

The B-25 bomber was named "Pauline" for a girlfriend of Charlie's (who
didn't wait for him). After the war, however, he met Carmen, to whom he
has been happily married for more than 70 years

Cover design by Matthew Lee Patek

Page design and production assistance by Adam Robinson for
GoodBookDevelopers.com

Printed in the United States of America

10 9 8 7 6 5 4 3 2 1

REMEMBERING THE CLOUD
THE TRUE STORY OF WWII PILOT
CHARLIE REDDIG

As Told To His Daughter

CONNIE KIRBY | MAJOR CHARLES REDDIG | DR. DENNIS DENENBERG

To the courageous men and women of
"The Greatest Generation" who defended freedom for all —
we thank YOU.

PROLOGUE

Daughter So, Dad, you really astonished the new doctor this morning with one of your answers to the health history questions she was asking.

Dad Which answer?

Daughter It was when she asked you, "Have you ever been exposed to radiation?" You said, "Well, 70 some years ago, I was flying my B-25 bomber returning from a raid on Tokyo, and we saw this enormous mushroom-shaped cloud in the sky over Hiroshima."

Dad Yes, and then I told her I lost a lot of hair over the next week or two; everyone on my crew did.

Daughter Then, you added that your hair grew back.

Dad That's when I saw the nurse looking at my head, and I told him it fell out again later, but that was due to age.

Daughter That's not the only unusual experience you have had in your life, Dad. I should interview you and write down some of these stories!

Dad You know where I live!

Contents

CHAPTER ONE

GROWING UP BEFORE THE WAR

Daughter Dad, I want to write down some of the stories you have told me over the years about your experiences flying B-25 bombers during WWII, but let's talk first about your experiences with airplanes before the war started. You grew up in the tiny village of Fivepointville, Pennsylvania, (which was named for five country roads coming together at one intersection). World War I had ended just six years before you were born, and airplanes had only been invented 11 years before that war started. What experiences did you have with airplanes growing up?

Dad My little school house had six grades all in one room, and when an airplane came within range of our hearing, classwork stopped, and everybody went to the windows, including the teacher, and we watched the airplane.

Daughter   You told me you learned to fly as a teenager. How did that come about?

Dad   My tiny hometown had a barbershop, a grocery store, a gas station, and two butchers. One of the butchers also owned the old Reading Airport which was just a grass strip, and he owned three airplanes or so. Anyway, I was good friends with his son John, and he asked John and me if we would like to learn to fly. I thought, "Oh yeah, why not, you know?" So, he taught us! After he thought we were good enough, he said, "Take the plane and go fly, but land back here—no place else, you hear me. Land back here."

We thought the gas tank was full, and John said, "You fly today." So I'm flying over Denver and Reamstown and Schoeneck (three small towns in Pennsylvania)—all over. It was a beautiful day. I'm up at about 5,000 feet, and the engine quits. John said, "It's all yours, Charlie."

I said, "I'll tell you what. I know every inch of those fields in Grandpop's farm; I'm going to try to put it down in the wheat field. There's no ditches, no rocks."

Daughter   So, when the engine quit, you just kept flying?

Dad   Yeah. You got to keep the nose down so you maintain speed. You can't just say, "Well I'm just going to sit here." Planes don't want to stay up in the air; they want to go down. If you keep the speed up, you have enough lift. And I was over Reamstown at the time. So I knew that I could glide it long enough to get it in the wheat field. I put it down in the field where the wheat was about knee high, walked up to Grandpop, and said, "We need some gas,"

"What for?" he said.

"For the airplane."

"An airplane! Where'd you get an airplane?"

"Ah, never mind, Grandpop. We need some gas."

We put gas in, and we pulled the tail back through the fence so I'd have a long enough run to take off because the thing is that next to the field is the Cocalico Creek and some pretty tall trees. And I only had so much room to take off; I couldn't go back further than the fence because I couldn't take the fence down. I revved up those engines, which weren't running full speed anyway because of the tractor gas, and held the brake there. Then I took off. John said he thinks the wheels clipped the trees; I don't think so. Anyhow, we made it. As we were going through the wheat field, though, the propeller was chopping off the top of the wheat, right, and the wheels are pulling wheat stalks out.

So, I get back to Reading, and I land the airplane. John's dad is standing out there, and the conversation goes like this:

John's dad: "Hey! What's that in the wheels?"

John and me: "Uhh…that's wheat. "

John's dad: "Where'd you get wheat in my airplane?"

Me: "Well, I landed ….."

John's dad: "Where were you all this time? You couldn't have stayed in the air this long? Where were you all this time?"

Me: "Well, the engine quit, and I landed in Grandpop's wheat field."

John's dad: "Where'd you get the gas to take off?"

Me: "From my grandfather."

John's dad: "You put tractor gas in my airplane and flew it?"

Me: "Yeah."

John's dad: "Well, alright, you can fly anytime you want to."

Daughter   And how old were you when this happened?

Dad   I was 13 or 14. I forget which. John was one year older than me. I remember that.

The tractor gas didn't have the octane that we really needed. John's dad had the mechanic drain the gas out afterward and put a higher-octane gas in it. John and I flew together a few times after that. We loved to fly that thing, but I never thought I'd be flying during a war.

Daughter So, Dad, how old were you when Pearl Harbor was attacked? What were your thoughts about the outbreak of war?

Dad I was 17. I was going to school at Wyomissing Poly Tech. They were teaching me to be a machinist, and they let me actually design and run different machines. I could have gotten a deferment because I was going to school. But I didn't. We had a bunch of guys in Stevens who played ball together, and we decided that we better help our country, you know, so we decided we're all going to sign up together. And most of us signed up at the same time. Some of us went together to Florida for basic training... infantry.

Daughter How old were you when you signed up?

Dad I went on my 19th birthday.

Daughter I thought you got your draft letter—that you were drafted.

Dad Yeah, we got our draft letters, but we decided to sign up before that. We decided as a ball team that we were going to go together, and we were going to fight together. We thought we were going to Germany. And, well, most of the rest of them did go to Germany.

CHAPTER TWO

TRAINING

Daughter So once you enlisted, what happened next?

Dad First, we went to Fort Indiantown Gap, but that wasn't training. All they did there was give us our clothing, our canteen, our boots, and the rest of our gear and sent us to basic training in St. Petersburg, Florida. I stayed at the Vinoy Hotel and slept on a cot in the ball room. The training was rough. I mean, for infantry, because we learned mortars, machine guns, and pistol firing. We crawled on the ground under barbed wire while they shot live ammunition over top of us. We ran an obstacle course where we had to do things like run, jump, and grab a rope that was hanging over a mud pit, and we had to swing across and not fall into the mud. We had to rappel off towers and run up a pyramid of logs and down the other side. One time, when we had gone all the way through the obstacle course, some general drives up and says, "I want to see the men go through the course!" Well, we were the only group there, so we went through it a second time. I thought I'd die. I really did.

Daughter   There's a picture of you in uniform with your family. I'm thinking that might have been taken between Indiantown Gap and Florida because once you were in Florida you didn't come home until the end of the war.

Dad   Right.

Daughter   OK, so in Florida you went through infantry training. And then?

Dad   And then we went to Fort Myers to train for shooting from an airplane. There was a pilot and a gunner in each plane with an open cockpit. We had a machine gun that swiveled up, down, left, and right; and there was another airplane towing a target. Each gunner had bullets with different colored tips. My tips were purple.

Daughter   What sort of target was it? I mean this was an actual plane flying with a target?

Dad   Yeah, the target plane had a long cable and behind that was a long circular sleeve. The air going through it kept it stretched out. That sleeve is what you had to hit. Anyway, my bullets made a purple mark when they went through the target. They would count these marks afterward because more than one plane shot at that target. Maybe some red marks were on that sleeve or some green ones, you know. I could actually see my bullets going into the target. Not many people can do that, but I could see them. You had to have so many marks on the sleeve to pass the course, right? And I'm putting them in, and this plane, by the way, is doing all kinds of maneuvers. I was pretty good with a machine gun. I knew I had more than enough hits, so I decided to shoot off the cable, and the cable fluttered down.

Daughter Did you get in trouble for doing that?

Dad They didn't know who did it.

Daughter Oh, because the bullet wasn't lodged anywhere, right?

Dad Right!

Daughter So this was your training at Fort Myers?

Dad Yes. It was called Fort Myers Gunnery School.

Daughter What happened after Fort Myers?

Dad   One day, they took us down the street with white handkerchiefs on our arms, and all day Friday we took tests. At 6:30 in the morning, I wasn't even sure I knew my name. Anyhow, there were all kinds of tests—everything you can think of. They brought us coffee and donuts, though. They let us go for lunch, and then we took tests in the afternoon. I was so tired of it; I thought, "Now it's over." Only, next day, there was half a day of tests again. They had everybody separated in this four-story building, and we took tests. Come Monday morning, we're out on the parade ground. I bet there were a thousand people out there. This, I think it was a captain or a major is down on the platform, and he says, "I'm looking for two men, Reddig and Quist. Report to the Orderly Room as soon as possible." I met the other guy, Quist, going in the door, and I said, "What did we do now?" The master sergeant there says, "You have 20 minutes to pack your things. We're going to put you on a train, and you can open up your orders then." They sent us to Scott Fields School to do radio navigation school.

Daughter   And where was that located?

Dad   Scott Field is in Illinois. That was a short course. Navigation school is where I came out of school one day and went down and looked at the bulletin board. It said that I had "KP[1]...no bunk tag." "What do you mean no bunk tag?" I knew I had put a tag with my name on my bunk before I went to class. So, I go into the Orderly Room. You're supposed to see the master sergeant, and he's supposed to schedule the time you go in to see the colonel. Well, I didn't know that. I go right in and open the door, and there are five high ranking officers in there, including the colonel. I said, "My name's Reddig, and I have a bunk tag on my bed, and I'm not going on KP!"

The sergeant comes flying in there; he says, "Oh my God."

This colonel was really nice. He said, "I wanna tell you how to report to an officer. I'm going to get you this little book here. You go out there and sit down and you read a couple pages and then you come in and report."

So, I read it. Then I said to the first sergeant, "My name is Reddig, I'd like to report to the officers in there." He says, "All right."

I knock on the door. "Come in."

"Reddig reporting, sir." I saluted, you know.

He says, "That was pretty good. I'll go with you to your room to see if you have a bunk tag." He does just that—all the way down to my barracks! I had the tag, but it was on the wrong end of my bunk, but the regulations didn't say which end it was supposed to be on, and I told him that. So, I went down to the bulletin board and scratched my name off of KP.

Daughter   And what was your rank at that time?

Dad   Private. I didn't know better, you know. I bet they laughed about that for years.

Daughter   And then?

Dad   We went back to Florida to Eglin Field where we trained to take off from a carrier. They had lines on the runway, and you had to have a full load. You had to lock the wheels and run the engines up as fast as they could go because you had to be in the air at that line on the runway. That's what we learned there.

Daughter   Maybe taking off that time when you were a teenager in your grandfather's wheat field and having to clear the tree tops was good practice for that!

Dad   Maybe so!

Daughter   What else do you remember about your time at Eglin Field?

Dad   I remember it rained like terrible. They used to have these wooden pallets that you walked on from building to building because the water was pretty deep. They said to us, "Don't ever take your hand and try to lift up a pallet because the snakes liked to hide underneath there." I never did care much for snakes.

Daughter Is Eglin where you met Baldasti?

Dad Yes, that's where we met the guys who later formed our crew.

Daughter But you didn't know they were going to be in your crew at that point. And he was the one who had flown before?

Dad Yeah, he told them he flew before, and they wouldn't let him be a pilot. He had to learn to take off and land like everybody else, though.

The question was, "Did you ever fly before?"

He said, "Yes, I have."

They said, "Well we can't use you because you might have learned things that you can't break; we want to train pilots to learn to fly our way."

They didn't ask me, and I didn't tell them. See, when I was thirteen, I'm flying, right? Now if they had asked me, I would have told them the truth, and then I would have never flown a bomber. I would have been just the navigator, but they didn't ask me, so I didn't offer the information.

Daughter Right, never volunteer information.

Dad Yeah, don't volunteer.

Daughter   What happened next?

Dad   Then they sent Lynn Quist and me to Greenville, South Carolina, where we learned to fly B-25s. They were hard instructors. Then, we flew to Suisun, California. There they painted my nice shiny airplane camouflage colors, but while we were there, a sand storm came up and took half the camouflage paint off my airplane; it wasn't dry, I guess. They had to paint it again.

From there, I flew it to a little island off the coast of California for refueling. Johnson Island it was called, and it was run by the Navy. I remember there was one tree on this whole island. There wasn't much to do for entertainment and we were there for a day and a half, and it was awfully hot, so Lynn Quist and I decided to go swimming even though there were signs that said "No Swimming." Anyway, we were swimming and suddenly I saw shark fins, and I yelled, "sharks," and Lynn and I swam as fast as we could back to the boat ramp, and we were still "swimming" up the concrete ramp because we were so scared. A bunch of sailors were watching us and laughing. After we got out, they told us that that those kinds of sharks rarely attack anyone. Lynn said to me, "You know, back home I have a whole shelf full of swimming trophies, but I didn't leave you behind even an inch!"

In Hawaii we practiced bombing a little island. Next to us was Schofield Barracks, an infantry place. That's where I saw my Grandpop's hired man. He was in the infantry, and he was at Schofield Barracks. I couldn't believe it. I'm carrying my parachute back to where we had a shack. You didn't lug it to your room or anything because we stayed in a hotel, which, by the way, they had built around the palm trees. In my room, there was the trunk of a tree going up through. Anyway, I saw the troops marching in. I've got pretty good eyes, you know, and I thought, "That can't be." If he wouldn't have been at the end of the row, I probably never would have seen him. Anyway, I saw this guy with sort of a limp because he had been in a bad accident one time. I recognized the way he walked, and I asked the sergeant, "Can you stop those men? I'd like to talk to somebody back there." He said "Sure." Sure enough, it was someone I knew. He said, "I'm in the Infantry". I said, "That's my plane down there." The next day I took him for a ride in my plane over Honolulu.

Dad Oh yeah. There was another guy one time who came up to me when I was taking my parachute back to the storage shack and asked if there was any chance of a ride. We were done bombing practice for the day, but I said I could take him tomorrow and told him what time. Well, we took him up for bombing practice, and when I asked him his name, he said, "DiMaggio." Here, it was Joe DiMaggio, a famous centerfielder for the New York Yankees. He was nicknamed "Joltin' Joe." He later married a famous movie star, Marilyn Monroe. Anyway, he went up with us. When we landed, he offered us tickets to a batting demonstration he was giving the next day, but we had to fly so we couldn't go.

Daughter Wow! Where did you go after Hawaii?

Dad Makin, in the Gilbert Islands.

Daughter So, from the time that you enlisted when you were 19, about how long before you were in Hawaii?

Dad I enlisted in 1943 on my birthday in February. In 1944, we're already in Hawaii practicing bombing.

Daughter So that was a year of training at all those different places.

Dad All those places- it was like three months here, a month there, and so on. Basic training down in Florida, radio navigation school at Scott Field, Illinois, flight training in Florida, carrier training in Florida, gunnery training in Ft. Myers-almost everything in Florida except for Illinois, you know.

Daughter And South Carolina?

Dad Yeah, in Greenville, SC, we got the bombers. Brand new bombers! I got a J-model then. I wanted the plane with the cannon, but I got the cannon later.

Daughter So, you were still in Hawaii on your 20th birthday.

Dad Yep.

Daughter How soon after that did you get to where you would be bombing real targets.

Dad Right away. We practiced bombing there for a short time and then went to the Gilberts.

Daughter OK. So, the Gilberts right after you turned 20 pretty much.

Dad Yeah.

Daughter What was life like at the various bases? Did you get homesick? Did you write letters home? How did you keep in contact with your parents?

Dad I used to write letters. They'd photograph them and make them small and then send them. Yeah, my Aunt Mary had a bunch of them. I wish she had given them to me. These were little things that were actually photographs of your letter.

Daughter Why did they do that?

Dad   Save space or something? I don't know. Also, the officers used to take turns reading the letters before they went out. Like I couldn't write, "Well today I'm on Okinawa." They would have scratched that out. "We bombed Truk today," would've been scratched out.

Daughter   The letters were censored.

Dad   Right. I was trying to think of that word.

Daughter   So, you wrote to your Aunt Mary. Was there anyone else you wrote letters to?

Dad   Oh, my parents, of course, yes. My youngest sister Rhonda used to write me letters, and that's about it.

Daughter   She was about 7, 8, 9?

Dad   Something like that.

Daughter   How often would you get mail?

Dad   Well, when we got 'em, we'd get a pretty nice pile because it used to take months sometimes before you'd get mail. On the Gilbert Islands we didn't get mail hardly at all because that was a desolate spot. Nobody had ever heard of these places! Think of those names like Truk, Maloelap, Kwajalein, Eniwetok. I'd never even heard of these places before, you know. These were all Japanese air bases. In fact, I never realized there were a lot of islands in the Pacific like that.

Daughter   What happened if you got sick?

Dad   It depended on where you were. In Hawaii there were hospitals, but when we were assigned to Okinawa, I flew the plane there and had a terrible pain in my abdomen. There were no hospitals or doctors. I asked around and someone said there was an army camp across the field, and they thought there was a medic. My crew found him. He had black marks on his face for camouflage since he was headed back into a combat area, and he was carrying a small medical kit about the size of a lunch box. He pushed on my side, and I passed out from the pain. He said I had appendicitis, and he thought he could do the operation because he had observed doctors doing it a couple of times.

Daughter   A medic isn't a doctor?

Dad   No, they have some medical training but aren't doctors. Anyway, I was in so much pain I didn't care what he did, so I laid down on a table in a tent, and he gave me a stick to bite on for the pain and asked if I wanted to watch. I said, "Sure, why not?" So he hung up a mirror so I could watch. He filled his helmet with soap and water and washed his hands real good and washed my stomach. Then, he took a knife, I guess it was a scalpel, and he cut me open and took out my appendix. He stitched me up and wrapped me up in bandages real good and said he had to get back to his unit.

Daughter What did you do?

Dad I went back to my plane and helped crank up some 500 pound bombs.

Daughter Did you tell anyone you had just had surgery?

Dad No way. They wouldn't have let me fly.

L-R Charles Reddig Jr, his younger sister Rhonda, his mother Carrie, his father Charles Reddig Sr., and his sister Marian. Charlie had picked up his uniform and other gear at Fort Indiantown Gap, and would shortly head for basic training in Florida. This was the last time he saw his family until he returned home after the war.`

CHAPTER THREE

THE MISSIONS

Daughter   What do you remember about the very first bombing raid you conducted? Do you remember the
date?

Dad   No, but I know it was Truk. They had more anti-aircraft. In fact, I think we lost three aircraft at Truk.

Daughter   Three out of how many? Out of how many airplanes?

Dad   About eighteen. It depended on how many you had
in the air.

Daughter   OK so you had about eighteen, and you lost 3
planes? You lost their crews too? Did any of them
escape?

Dad   When you lose the plane, you lose everything.

Daughter And your plane was hit?

Dad Yeah. It was hit many times, many times.

Daughter On that first raid?

Dad Oh yeah, I remember we had two holes on that first raid because the ground crew gave us heck for it; they had to patch them up, you know.

Daughter Were you the pilot or the navigator for that first raid?

Dad Co-pilot on the first raid.

Daughter When you were hit, did you…?

Dad You don't realize it. You hear something hitting. Then, you get on the intercom and say, "Anyone hit back there?" "No, a couple holes." You check on your men; I checked on my men. If nobody was hit, you just keep on doing your job, you know. Now, if they would have hit the gas tank or something, I would have probably tried to make it home. Because when you hit the gas tank, a lot of fuel goes out pretty fast.

Daughter   It doesn't explode?

Dad   No, no. You just lose fuel. We did have an airplane on fire once, and we had to jump.

Daughter   So from your base to this, on this first mission, about how long was that?

Dad   Maybe a 45-50-minute flight one way. Truk was a place they really wanted to hit because Truk had a lot of Betty Bombers on it. They were the ones who were bombing our troops all over the place. Japan had the Betty Bombers. You want to hit the bombers because they kept us awake at night too. You couldn't sleep. Boom! Boom! Boom! One time, they hit the bomb dump. We called the place where the bombs were stored the bomb dump. It blew. It was like an earthquake. I mean, we were down in this hole and the dirt's falling down on us. I mean, everything is shaking. That was a lucky hit; they really hit that.

Daughter   What was the plane on that first mission?

Dad   Always a B-25. But this one was a J, and I had the machine guns. I didn't have the cannon in this one; it had a glass nose with machine guns.

Daughter   How many bombs did it carry?

Dad   Six 500 pounders. Six bombs and two machine guns, four rockets on each wing. And I think it had twelve 50-caliber machine guns— about twelve in the J model.

Daughter   Twelve machine guns? And how many people were manning those? I mean there are five people in the plane.

Dad   The co-pilot (if we had one) or I fired the forward firing guns, and the top turret gunner fired the top turret. The navigator/radio man fired the two waist guns, and the tail gunner fired two in the tail.

Daughter   So everybody, all crew members…

Dad   Oh yeah. We all had to go to gunnery school and learn how to shoot. You had to do it blindfolded— even take them apart blindfolded. When I finished school, I knew the machine gun inside and out. They gave you a 50 caliber, and they blindfolded you. You took it apart piece by piece, and if there was something wrong, you told the instructor, "This piece is worn" or "I can't find the firing pin; it's missing." If they gave you a machine gun that was set up so the bullets came in on the right side, then blindfolded you had to make the bullets come in on the left side; you had to change the feed. You then had to take it to the range, and it better fire or you flunked. So, we knew that machine gun inside and out. That instruction was just perfect there. First, they taught us, don't get me wrong, what to look for and to feel the parts so that we knew what each part did and could put it back together. My tail gunner was really good, too. One time, his guns jammed back there. To unjam it, you put the asbestos gloves on and you have to unscrew the barrel and drop it in the ocean and screw the barrels back in and set the proper head space and get it firing. I swear he was back shooting both guns again in under five minutes. I had a good crew. They knew what they were doing.

Daughter You mentioned the tail gunner. What were the other positions on the crew?

Dad There was the tail gunner, a top turret gunner, a pilot, a co-pilot, and a waist gunner.

Daughter Two pilots?

Dad If one's killed, you've sacrificed everyone; whereas if you have a co-pilot you might be able to get them down. Sometimes, the pilot would get killed, and the co-pilot would put him out of the seat and take over. He didn't have to take the pilot's seat, you know, you have dual controls exactly alike.

Daughter In a B-25?

Dad Oh yeah. I would use my right hand to do the throttle, and he sat over here. He would use his left hand to control the throttle. You can control the plane from both seats. Otherwise, you'd have to leave your seat, un-strap him, and get him out of there somehow. With dual controls, you just stayed in your seat, and you could take control of the plane.

Gordon Leslie Furst was the tail gunner. John Baldasti was the top turret. Lynn Quist for a while was co-pilot, and then he got his own plane. Stacey was the pilot in the very beginning. I flew with him for the first time. Then, he and another guy, Turville, both got killed. From then on, I got to fly.

Daughter What was your rank at this point?

Dad Sergeant first class. And so was Lynn Quist. We were both sergeant first class. I guess we were the only two flying sergeants.

Daughter Oh. So everybody else flying was....?

Dad Either a second lieutenant or a sergeant. We weren't really going to be pilots. We were pushed into it. They said, "Since you've had the training, would you like to actually fly a bomber?" Oh yeah, why not, you know. Better than navigating, so we flew.

Daughter You once said you never lost a crew member, but Stacey was killed.

Dad   That was not my crew.

Daughter   What was your crew?

Dad   My crew was the only crew that came home alive out of, well… at one time we had about 28 planes. They didn't all fly at the same time; there was always some broken down. Most of the times, when we went to China, I think we had maybe 14 planes in the air because it was a job to put extra fuel tanks in. I don't know how they did it. I wasn't there. They had to put extra tanks in above the bomb bay because you could crawl through the bomb bay back to the tail, you know. That's the space they used to put some kind of fuel tanks in. Then, we had to leave one bomb behind so we had the fuel there and back.

Daughter   So you had a tail gunner, Leslie Gordon Furst, and he was with you the whole time?

Dad   Yeah, Oh yeah. And John Baldasti who had the top turret.

Daughter   And Lynn Quist was there the whole time? Who else?

Dad   "Rossi" Rossetti was the navigator and waist gunner, but don't ask me his first name. I just remember we always called him "Rossi."

Daughter Um, and your jobs were sometimes pilot, sometimes navigator, sometimes gunner?

Dad You see they tried to give a lot of different people pilot training because we were short of pilots, really short. That's how we got to be pilots because there was a shortage. Sometimes, there was no co-pilot. There just weren't enough pilots. Everyone in the crew had learned to fly, so if something happened to the pilot, and there was no co-pilot, another crew member would have had to crawl over the bomb bay, somehow get the pilot out of the way, and take the controls. Anyway, that crew, let's say after 10 missions, was the crew that stayed together.

Daughter So how did it feel on that first mission? Were you scared?

Dad If people say they weren't scared, they're crazy. You're scared, but you do your job. Things happen so fast when you're over the target. You really don't have time to be scared. What you realize is that you've got four other men with you, right, and their lives depend on you, too. You better do your job the best you can and not sit there and be scared. So you do your job. Afterwards, you might say, "Boy, that was close" or "They had a lot of anti-aircraft down there," or "A lot of flak (case fragments from exploding weapons) flying around up there." We would discuss it among ourselves after.

Daughter You had to be exhausted when you got back.

Dad Yeah, it was a mental exhaustion, you know. What you were trying to do, of course, is dodge when the flak is coming up. If you saw that they had a pattern, you either tried to change altitude or change direction to get out of that pattern to make the gunner down there change his shooting. That's what I'm doing all the time; I'm trying to maneuver to keep the guy down there from making a direct hit. When you are over the target, though, you've got to fly straight and level especially when you are dropping a torpedo. When you drop a torpedo and they're shooting at you, you can't say, "Oh, I'm going to get away from these guys shooting at me." You have to be straight and level and drop the torpedo. Then, you can peel off. The torpedo has to hit the water just right, or it will veer off. That's a very dangerous mission.

Daughter So that's more difficult than bombing a land target.

Dad Yeah, you got to get pretty close.

Daughter And you had both kinds of targets on every mission? Did you have ships and land targets on every mission?

Dad They were separate missions. The torpedoes are hanging under the plane. You didn't want to put bombs in the bomb bay and accidentally have the bomb drop down on the torpedo and blow everything up. Besides the weight of that torpedo is about all the plane can handle.

Daughter   So you only had a torpedo when you were going after Japanese ships.

Dad   Oh yeah, one torpedo. You drop it, and you get the heck out of there. Start going home.

Daughter   I think at one point you told me you flew a total of sixty-nine missions.

Dad   At least half of those were over Tokyo. We bombed Japan more than anything else. I'd say half of them were bombing all these different islands and probably half of them bombing Japan though we bombed Okinawa a lot, too. We had to help take Okinawa. We used to load up with bombs, drop them, come back, load up, drop 'em, just round robin.

Daughter   Did each one count as a mission?

Dad   Each one was a mission. A mission is a landing and a take-off. It wasn't 69 days. It was 69 flights, yeah, even if you had a malfunction. Say you left to go to the target and the right engine went out and you turned home to come back, that's still a mission. We didn't have to do that often— come home.

Daughter   There was no GPS back then. How did you navigate? How could you figure out where you were?

Dad   OK, here's how it worked. Up top is a rotating antenna. It picks up radio stations, frequencies from different stations. On a map, I marked out 360 degrees, looks like a big clock. I tune in Hawaii. Hawaii says 270 degrees. I draw a line 270 degrees on the map, right.

Daughter   And when you say you tuned in to Hawaii?

Dad   My antenna is pointing right at Hawaii. I turn this antenna to get the strongest signal. The antenna is showing me where it's pointing down here on this dial. The antenna says 270 degrees, so I draw a line, right? Now, I get China, and China is 90 degrees so I draw a line. I'm right here where those 2 lines cross. I get a third station over here someplace, and now I know exactly where I'm going, where I'm heading. From there, I can tell the pilot, "If you want to hit Nagasaki, go 300 degrees."

Daughter   Ok, are you drawing like with a pencil on this map?

Dad   With a pencil, yeah, on the map.

Daughter   Now, you've taken another reading. Do you have multiple pencil marks? That would be a lot of crisscrossed lines.

Dad   Sure, yeah, yeah. I could erase them because I have a pencil.

Daughter   These stations that are broadcasting, are these from military bases?

Dad   No, I listened to Tokyo Rose[2] a lot. She had the latest American Music. I loved to listen to her.

Daughter   So, these regular broadcasts helped you find your target?

Dad   Yeah.

Daughter   How often did you recalculate?

Dad   Maybe every 15 to 20 minutes. 'Cause you're doing a couple hundred miles an hour. Oh, by the way, there was a trailing wire that came out the bottom of the airplane. It was a hunk of lead which looked like a big egg, and hanging from it was a cable. This was my antenna. This thing hangs down, and you have to run it up and down until you get the strongest signal. If your station is too weak, it won't know the exact direction. So you put this down till you get the strongest signal. Now, you know you're going to be accurate 'cause that's where that station is. When you land, you better pull that thing back up again because you don't want it to get caught in wires or something like that. It was called the trailing wire antenna. We all learned this in navigation school.

Daughter Even though the five crew members survived the war, did you ever lose a plane?

Dad Oh yeah…yeah. We had the right engine on fire coming back from Japan, and I smelled fuel. I don't know why it didn't blow. I told the guys we were going to have to jump. They jumped. Then, I jumped last. The plane kept on going for a while, and we parachuted into the water. A PBY came, and, by the way, a Japanese ship must have got the radio message. It was coming out to pick us up.

Daughter What's a PBY?

Dad A PBY is a flying boat, a seaplane, but don't ask me what the letters stood for. Anyway, one at a time, they picked us out of the water and got us away from that ship, or we'd have been prisoners of war.

And I lost another plane when I couldn't get the landing gear down. Nobody was hurt there, and I brought it in on one wheel. Well, actually, I tried to break the wheel off, the one that was down. You can't do it. That plane bounces. The wheel was so strong that the plane just bounced up in the air. I figured I can't break it off, so I'm going to have to land on one wheel, and I came in on one wheel. Of course, the wing was badly damaged because the plane spins around. The propeller was bent, and that messes up the engine. We all got out, but we lost that airplane. Once the wing hits, you can't take a chance on flying it you know. That was the end of that one, but I got the H model after that with a cannon.

Daughter So that was a more advanced model then the J.?

Dad Well, it had a 75-millimeter cannon which was a very good weapon. I used to hit tanks and stuff with that; it was really good except for the fact that it made me cry.

Daughter It made you cry?

Dad Yeah, the smoke was so bad from firing that cannon that it burned my nose and my eyes.

Daughter So, half your missions were on the islands where the Japanese were stationed?

Dad I'd say about half were on the different islands. The other half were the main land, the major island, Japan itself.

   I remember we were never ever allowed to bomb the Emperor's castle. It's good we didn't try because we had photographs of it. Boy, he had anti-aircraft guns, rings of them around there. I don't think we would have made it over and back if we would have tried. They really protected him.

Daughter So, you were stationed at two different bases. How many missions out of the Gilberts versus how many missions out of Okinawa?

Dad Oh, I'd say maybe half and half. I wish I had a list; I used to have a list of them- like so many times Truk, so many times Eniwetok, so many times Wotge. We had a list of how many missions we did on each one.

Daughter Even if you didn't lose planes, you sometimes came back with bullet holes, right?

Dad Oh yeah, I brought it back with holes in it, and the ground crew had to patch them up. They didn't like that so they used to say, "Can't you stay away from these anti-aircraft? We've got to patch all these holes." You see, I didn't own the airplane; the ground crew "owned" it. In their opinion, I only borrowed it to fly it. They would use a beat-up airplane, a wrecked one, and cut the aluminum out and then patch them up. One time, they told us we had 70 holes, something like that. Nobody was hit. The radio was shot out. I mean the radio was worthless, and that would be replaced.

Daughter And wasn't somebody's canteen shot one time?

Dad   That was John Baldasti. He was in the top turret, and this shrapnel came up behind my seat, up into the top turret. I don't know what he had in the canteen. It might have been beer for all I knew. In fact, I think it was beer.

He was a Catholic boy. I had never heard him swear before, but he was swearing. I heard him on the intercom. I thought, "Something's really wrong here." I got on the intercom and said "John, what's the matter up there?"

He yelled, "You ought to see my canteen!"

"Why do I want to see your canteen"

"Well, you ought to see it! When we get down on the ground, I'll show it to ya!"

When we got down, I see that the shrapnel had gone inside the canteen and stayed in there. You could hear it rattling around. Whatever was in it, of course, ran out the bottom and down the bottom of the airplane and went out there. He was perturbed, so I'm sure it wasn't water. He had to get a new canteen.

CHAPTER FOUR

MEETING HEADHUNTERS

Daughter Dad, you have told us about a very interesting person you met, a real headhunter! How did you meet him?

Dad When we first landed in the Gilbert Islands, these island people were afraid of us because the Japanese had treated them terribly. The Japanese didn't come by airplane; they came by ships and submarines to take Makin. The island people had really never seen airplanes. So here we come with these big bombers. By the way, the Sea Bees[3] laid our runway. Anyway, here we come with these big bombers, making all kinds of noise, and they're afraid. We saw them behind the trees watching us so we decided to wave to them. We'd just go about our business and just wave to them. I guess the chief's son was a little braver than the rest of them. I didn't know at the time he was the chief's son, but he was. One time, he got close to the airplane, and I put my hand up, and he said, "Chitabu!" Well, alright…Chitabu. I pointed to myself and said "Charlie!" He goes, "Chitabu, Charlie. Chitabu, Charlie." That's how we met. I did learn a couple words. Something that sounded like "kunimari" was a sort of greeting; I learned that from him. He learned to say OK; after that everything was "Ok." I gave him a candy bar.

One morning, he's sitting by the end of the tent peg, waiting for me to wake up. He had probably watched us eat coconuts because they watched everything we did from behind the trees. He had this big machete, and he had like twine wrapped around like a belt to hold this machete at his side. When I wake up, he goes up the tree. I mean they practically run up those trees. I tried to climb a coconut tree once. I took skin off a couple of places; I was a bloody mess when I came down. I only did it once. They would practically just run up those trees. Anyway, he gets a couple green coconuts in his arm, chops them off, and using just one arm to hold on, he comes back down. He took the coconut and chopped the top off with his machete and handed it to me. Well, I drank it; it was really good.

Daughter   Where would he have gotten a machete?

Dad   Captain Cook! They know that Captain Cook in the 1700's traded sail cloth and machetes and stuff for fresh water and papaya from the native people.

Every morning, unless it was ugly weather, Chitabu would be out there, and he'd go up the trees as soon as I woke up and get me coconuts. Every time I got some chocolate bars, I'd give him one. He loved them.

Daughter What did he wear?

Dad Well, it was like a rope, with like a thong thing. Now, the kids didn't wear anything. They were very healthy and ate a lot of fish. It was almost like a paradise there. They had orchids growing wild; they had bread fruit, papaya, two kinds of bananas, and all kinds of fish and monkeys.

Daughter You had said that Chitabu didn't live on that island?

Dad Oh no. I had to swim to his island. He lived on another island. Yeah.

Daughter About how far was that?

Dad About a half mile.

Daughter So, you swam a half mile?

Dad Yeah, with my 45. I had a little fishing line, and I had my Zippo lighter.

Daughter How'd you keep those dry?

Dad The 45 got wet, but I wrapped the lighter in plastic from the cigarette pack. That's how I kept the lighter dry. It got a little wet anyway, but it worked when I used it finally.

Daughter So why did you swim over to the other island?

Dad I wanted to visit him. I swam over and there's two guys out there watching me swim. I put my hand up and said, "Chitabu." They talked among themselves. Then, they motioned for me to come. I heard these sounds like thumping. When we came to this village, there's nobody there—nobody. The whole village is empty. Their huts were built up on tree stumps. They had this long log chopped with steps going up to the entrance, and they motioned for me to go up there. Inside there's a chief and a guy on each side of him.

I couldn't talk to them, but as I was going through the jungle, I was clicking on the cigarette lighter, and I got it to work. I looked at the chief, and he looked at me and I looked at him. Finally, I said, "Chitabu." He said "Ah, ah." I don't know if this was the father or not, but they knew who Chitabu was. When I clicked my lighter, he sort of jumped back. Then, I went real close and gave it to him. He did it, and it worked. He was amazed. I let him keep it.

I also had this little ball of fishing line. They had to make their own fishing line. The women would twist this stringy stuff that grew there and make fishing line. Well, this was nylon fishing line. I gave it to him. He tried to tear it, and he couldn't. Boy, he got the biggest smile. He knew right away that this would be good fishing line.

Then he talked to the guards, and when I came down the steps, the whole village was alive. Kids were running all over the place, even wild boar. Everybody was there. They must have given the signal that the coast was clear. I bet I wasn't in there for 15 or 20 minutes, but I'm tired. I had swum, and then I had to go a long way with these guys to this village, and now I had to go to another village. The jungle grows fast, and, every now and then, they were slashing at undergrowth to give me a path to go through.

As we neared the next village, Chitabu saw me coming. He jumped up in the air and yelled. He gets the family together. The whole village thought this is the greatest. Then, of course, they build me a bed. They had these big like banana leaves, and they had all kinds of stuff like branches, and they built this thing up and put sailcloth on the top. I think I slept on a piece of sailcloth from Captain Cook when they made that bunk for me. I really do. So, I'm tired and I figure I have my 45 but I gotta sleep no matter what. The chief must have sent a guy to guard me. He sat with a machete in his hand all night. I woke up the next morning with the sun shining in my face, and the guy's still sitting there. They fed me. I don't know what I ate, but I licked the salt rock, and I did what they did. Thank goodness, I didn't have to swim back. Chitabu took me back on the outrigger that he built.

His outrigger, which had a sail by the way, was hollowed out of a log. When he was bringing me back to my island on this beautiful sunny day, I noticed we're getting pretty far off-shore. I thought that was pretty funny because he was supposed to be taking me home, and home wasn't out in the water. Suddenly, he dove overboard and left me sitting in there. I took a deep breath; he's not up. I took another deep breath. Now, I was in good shape, but he still wasn't up. I'm wondering if I should dive in, or if I should try to use this sail which I knew nothing about and still today I know nothing about sailing. I think I had taken a third breath when he popped up with a big smile on his face, and he's hiding something. I wanted to see what it was, but he wouldn't show me, and he hid it. He took me back. I got off the boat and waved goodbye. He knelt in the sand. I see him digging, and he puts something in the sand. It was a shell. He knew that the ants would eat the insides out of that shell while it was in the sand. After the ants ate the inside out, he polished it with coconut husk and gave it to me. It was a beautiful cowrie shell, and I still have it.

Daughter Is that the only time you visited his island?

Dad Yes. Oh, it was too far. I mean, once was enough. He was over at my island all the time.

Daughter So most of the time he came over to your island.

Dad Oh my, yes. He was there almost every morning.

Daughter Did you let someone know you were going to Chitibu's island because wouldn't they have worried that you were gone overnight?

Dad My tail gunner—I told my tail gunner I'm going.

Daughter You have always said they were headhunters. How did you know that?

Dad There was a missionary on the island who had been trying to teach them not to behead their enemies. I don't know if he had made any progress, but I did see two of the men in Chitabu's village each carrying around a shrunken head.

Daughter If you could meet Chitabu today, what would you want to say to him? (Assuming you could find someone to translate!)

Dad I would ask, "What did you feed me?" And "Where did you get sailcloth? Do your people have stories about Captain Cook?

Daughter   You also told us about a pet you had on that island.

Dad   Yes, I had a pygmy monkey.

Daughter   How did you get him as a pet?

Dad   Every time we lost a man, we got a double shot of whiskey. I found an empty bottle and instead of drinking whiskey in a hundred degrees of heat, I saved it. I saved enough whiskey to make a full fifth. This sailor came with a monkey. I don't know where he came from; it doesn't really matter. The little monkey jumps over to my shoulder. I thought he was pretty cute, you know. I should have left him alone; I should have let the sailor keep him.

Instead, I said, "Boy, he's pretty nice."

The sailor said, "What do you got to trade for the monkey?"

"Umm...whiskey?"

"You got whiskey?"

I said, "Yes, I have a fifth of whiskey".

He said, "You got the monkey."

I gave him the whiskey, and now I got the monkey. The monkey was naughty. He opened up and exposed all my film. Once, he broke up all the cigarettes and made a pyramid out of three cartons of cigarettes. He used to clean the lizards out of our beds, though. He had one good job, so we forgave everything because he would clean out the lizards and throw them out on the floor.

Daughter What was his name?

Dad I forget. I called him "naughty" most of the time. I used to say, "You're a naughty monkey." Then he'd cover his face. He was a smart little fellow. Once, he fell out of a tree. He had this scrunched-up face, and he's rubbing his backside. I wish I had taken a picture of him. I didn't think a monkey would ever fall out of a tree, but he did.

Another thing I remember was one time I had the monkey on my shoulder; he liked to sit there, and I was walking along and all of a sudden I saw a guy shaving, and he had a large mirror setting at the tent peg while he was shaving using water in his steel helmet. The monkey saw the mirror, and he jumped down to get the other monkey. He went through all kinds of gyrations trying to get the other monkey. He got on top of the mirror to reach down; he ran around it, and he finally got so tired I had to take the mirror away so he wouldn't have a heart attack. I don't know if the guy ever finished shaving, we were all laughing so hard.

Daughter What happened to him?

Dad At the end of the war, I wanted to take him home, but they said he had to have some kind of shot. They gave him the shot, and it killed him. I think they called it a distemper shot. He was such a small monkey, and I guess they gave him too much. He didn't survive.

Daughter That's sad, but my grandmother wouldn't have appreciated having a naughty monkey in her house. Just sayin'!

Dad True.

A monkey similar in appearance to the "naughty monkey" Charlie had as a pet during WWII. He has no actual photographs because "Naughty Monkey" opened all the film canisters Charlie's parents had sent and played with the rolls like yo-yos, thus exposing the film and ruining it.

CHAPTER FIVE

AUGUST 6, 1945:
THE FINAL MISSION

Daughter On the morning of August 6, 1945 –

Dad That was a bad day for Japan.

Daughter You were the navigator for a mission to bomb targets in Tokyo. What do you recall about that mission?

Dad Well, when we left and flew over Hiroshima, it was a city, a thriving city.

Daughter What did you see when you flew over it on the way to Tokyo?

Dad I saw buses and taxis and trains – everything you would see in like the city of Lancaster (a small city in Pennsylvania near Charlie's hometown) and we went to go bomb Tokyo. On the way back, we didn't know anything about atomic bombs; nobody had told us anything.

Daughter What base were you on at this point?

Dad Okinawa. We were going to return to Okinawa, and um…I think it was Baldasti in the top turret. I think he was the one who said, "Are we lost?" I was looking up. I was always looking for Zeros,[4] always, because they attack you from above and never from under, and they always come out of the sun. So I'm looking for Zeros, and I'm not looking down at the ground. Baldasti says again, "Are we lost?", and I said "What do you mean, 'Are we lost?'"

"Well, look down there."

I put the nose down. What I saw made me think I was lost. The city was gone. Fires burned everywhere, and there was a big black cloud in the air. It looked like H-E-L-L. If someone would've asked me, "describe it in one word," that would be the closest. Every now and then, there were pieces of wall standing. There used to be a place called Shuri Castle, and it was no longer there. A big solid castle—even that was gone. We thought "what in the world?" We wondered if it was an earthquake possibly because we couldn't understand what would have caused all the fires and destruction. Later, we found out that the world's first atomic bomb had been dropped.

Daughter How did you find that out? Did they make an announcement?

Dad I think it was Tokyo Rose on the radio who told us, I think it was her.

Daughter Nobody at the base said to you, "Charlie…"

Dad The base didn't know what went on. We saw it. We actually saw it.

Daughter How low were you over Hiroshima at that point, roughly?

Dad Maybe a thousand feet.

Daughter You were that low? You really were exposed to the radiation.

Dad Oh yeah. I used to worry about that later because then I had learned more about radiation. Of course, I was doing a couple of hundred miles an hour, and it wasn't long until I was well past it, but I still worried.

We tried to tell other guys what we saw, but they didn't see it, so, they didn't know what we were talking about. I kept saying, "The city is gone, virtually gone!"

"Come on Charlie, come on."

"It is," I said. "There's fires all over the place, and most of the buildings are just leveled. Even the train tracks are gone!"

The heat, evidently, turns the steel tracks into dust. That's all I can figure because they weren't there anymore.

Daughter   And that was particularly noticeable to you because I remember you saying you often followed the train tracks.

Dad   Oh yes, we followed tracks to bases. We bombed terminals and stuff like that because they moved a lot of their stuff, of course, by rail. The soldiers back at the base didn't know what we were talking about. I don't think they believed us until they heard this on the radio. Then I guess they sort of got the idea.

Daughter   Was it the same day that they heard it on the radio?

Dad   Oh yeah, we landed, and of course we had to put our stuff away, put our parachutes away, and refuel the airplane. You do all kinds of stuff to get ready for the next mission. Of course, you're only with your crew there. We were working on our airplane so we were discussing the city as we had seen it. Every now and then, we'd see somebody else and tell them what we saw. They all said, "Well what do you mean, 'The city is gone?'"

I'm pretty sure it was Tokyo Rose on the radio who said, "We were bombed today and that..." She didn't call it an atomic bomb. I don't think they knew what hit 'em. I really don't. She said, how did she put that? "Today our city is no longer like it was, and we're not quite sure what happened, but we think it was bombed." She didn't mention "atomic" because I don't think they knew.

Daughter The pictures of the mushroom cloud, you were actually seeing that cloud?

Dad On my right. Many years later, in fact, just a few years ago, I met a guy who came to swim at the rec center, and he had seen it on his left, so we were both coming back to Okinawa. He said he was in a B-24 coming back from Japan, and he saw the thing on his left. I saw it on my right so we must have been only miles apart.

Daughter Any guesses as to how soon after the bomb exploded that you were in the area?

Dad The cloud hadn't dissipated yet, but I don't know when it exploded. We were all the way up north in Japan, and we didn't know a thing about it, and where we were it didn't bother us at all.

Daughter So now, you're flying south.

Dad Now, we're flying south, and all of a sudden, we see the cloud first and then we looked down and........ what happened, what happened to the city? When we passed over it, it was a city.

Daughter You had flown that flight pattern to get to Tokyo; there's Hiroshima, but, now you're coming back, and it's gone.

Dad We had never seen anything like that. What really amazed me was the railroad tracks. Now, think of the temperature it has to take to melt railroad tracks. It wasn't that it just melted them because they could have been seen if they were still there, but they were gone. That means they disintegrated. They said it was hotter than the sun, the bomb. That's what I was told.

Daughter How far were you from the cloud do you think? I mean you didn't fly through it, did you?

Dad No, we flew alongside it; I don't know how far. Oh, maybe from here to the house across the street.

Daughter Wow, you were really close to that cloud!

Dad And it still had that-I'm going to call it a mush-room-sort of a mushroom shape. It was dissipating. I mean, it wasn't gone. I could still tell what it looked like. I could clearly see it as a mushroom cloud.

Daughter You had talked about, prior to your flight, you were somewhere, and there was a plane being guarded.

Dad Yeah, Tiniman Island close to the Philippines was where it took off from.

Daughter Why would you have been in the Philippines'?

Dad I took the nurses there to get medical supplies because of a terrible storm we had that blew away all our tents and supplies.

Daughter And you saw a plane that was being guarded.

Dad We landed there, and we got coffee from the Red Cross. Far out there in the field, there was an airplane, and something was on the ground covered up. A whole bunch of guys were standing around it with machine guns. That's all I know. We thought afterwards that it could have been the atomic bomb. It was a B-29, and this thing was on the ground. It was pretty big. I could tell what kind of airplane it was, and I could tell there was something on the ground covered up that they were guarding. That's all I know. When we got talking about it later on, we thought it might have been the atomic bomb. We might have seen it before it was dropped.

Daughter Did you have any physical effects from being that close to the cloud?

Dad We lost some of our hair. Our whole crew did. I'd comb my hair, and it would fall out. A lot of it dropped out for, oh, maybe a few weeks, but it came back again.

Daughter Did you connect that in your mind to the cloud?

Dad No, I didn't. I never knew much about radiation. A couple of the nurses were telling people that we did get a lot of radiation by flying close to that bomb.

Daughter You didn't get nauseous or sick or anything, just lost hair?

Dad No. I guess we were through it too fast, which is good.

Daughter Did you think the atomic bomb meant the end of the war? Were you thinking you might soon be on your way home?

Dad Well, three days later, they dropped the second one on Nagasaki. That's when we thought, "Well, we might be going home." We really couldn't put two and two together on the first one, but then we heard the reports on the second one, and what the Emperor said.[5]

Daughter That day was your last combat action, but you didn't know it until the Japanese announced their unconditional surrender on Aug. 15. What was your feeling when the news of the surrender came?

Dad I couldn't believe that our missions were over.

Daughter That mushroom cloud mission was your last mission?

Dad That was our last mission actually. That was it, but we didn't know that. When they announced that the war was over, people started shooting all over Okinawa, shooting stuff in the air. Baldasti went out to the plane and pulled the emergency release and dropped six bombs on the runway. They didn't go off, thank goodness!

Then we thought we were going to fly our new planes home. We had gotten brand new bombers just before that, brand spankin' new! Ha! HA! The joke was on us. They put us on the Sea Flyer ship and we spent 28 days on the water. We finally came up the Columbia River. As for the new plane, I heard they sawed the tails off all the planes.

Daughter Why did they saw the tails off?

Dad We were never told. There were a lot of rumors, like they didn't want future enemies to get hold of them, or that it would be too expensive to bring them back when they weren't really useful for civilian purposes like freight or passengers, but we never found out.

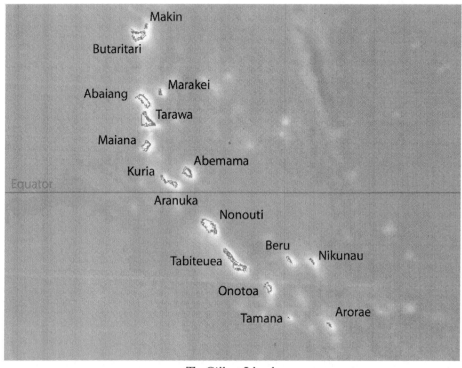

The Gilbert Islands

Charlie in uniform

*For basic training in St. Petersburg, Florida soldiers were billeted at
the Vinoy Hotel where Charlie slept on a cot in the ball room*

Charlie playing baseball on Makin Island

Charlie and Baldasti in Honolulu—
palm trees in rooms of our hotel

Foolish me, I scraped off lots of skin
trying to climb a palm tree

My turn cranking up 500 pound bombs to
drop on Japanese island strongholds

Loading up to give presents to Hirohito, 1945 Okinawa
(Hirohito was Emperor of Japan)

Charlie in Okinawa

Lynn Quist on right, Charlie on left. Lynn was a champion speed swimmer, but we both swam equally fast when we saw shark fins while swimming off Johnson Island.

PAULINE # 33975

Our first plane—B-25

One of my 50 caliber guns as we are going to bomb nearby Japanese islands

Ready for high altitude—looks hot, huh? But the air at altitude was cold so these were necessary even in the tropical climate.

Okinawa—captured Japanese suicide plane

Home at present—this tent was "home away from home"

Me - Makin (Island) - our tent

I can't read this sign—we took over the island & they left this here

Runway on Makin in the Gilberts

This is John Baldasti in the B-25 bomber.

I fly today to Tokyo. Inspection of aircraft both inside and outside ... controls, ammo, bombs, fuel, chutes, life rafts, etc.

The tent in Okinawa had a wooden floor

Flying from Oahu to the Gilbert Islands

A small section of the supply ships ring around Okinawa harbor

CHAPTER SIX

COMING HOME

Daughter   How soon after the Aug. 15 surrender announcement were you told you would be coming home?

Dad   Maybe a week.

Daughter   So, you boarded the ship probably in August.

Dad   Yeah, it was hot, and we had to climb up a rope ladder to get on the ship. The food was good on the
ship, really good. We even had ice cream. I slept
in a lifeboat, so did Lynn Quist. If we would have
gone down where the guys were sick, we would
have been sick too.

Daughter   You stayed in the fresh air.

Dad   One day, we were hungry. We went down to eat and
there was no line. We got down a few more steps to

the mess hall where the chief cook is, and he's sick. He said, "Help yourself to anything you want. My boys are all sick; take what you want." We really ate that day!

Daughter   I wonder why they were all sea sick? These were sailors, and they would have gone through the whole war on ships, right?

Dad   Out in the middle of the ocean, the dumb engines blew. The boat's going like this…whomp…whomp. That gets you.

    That's when Lynn Quist dove over the side and decided to swim under the ship and come up the other side.

Daughter   Why?

Dad   He told me he was gonna do it. I said, "You're crazy. You know how much ship there is down under the water?" He was a champion swimmer. He had trophies from speed swimming and everything else. Well, he made it, but just barely. On the other side, he came up the rope ladder all bloody from being scraped by the barnacles on the ship. Anyhow, we did swim in the middle of the ocean, he and I. We asked the captain. It was stinking hot and the boat's not going anywhere. The dolphins were swimming all over the place. The captain said, "As long as the dolphins are out there, you may swim. If the dolphins leave, you get out of there." They threw garbage overboard, and the sharks would come in a frenzy. We put this rope ladder down. We didn't swim away from the ship; the dolphins were right with us, so we did swim a little bit in the ocean.

Daughter OK, so the war was over August 15, 1945. You said you were on the ship for—

Dad 28 days.

Daughter You actually weren't home, then, until end of September, early October. Where did you land in the US?

Dad Up the Columbia River, Oregon, Camp Rilea. R-I-L-E-A, I believe.

Daughter From there, how did you get home to Pennsylvania?

Dad You see this is where I'm blank. I guess we came home by train, but—isn't that funny, that's the part I don't remember— how I got home. That's awful. I mean I know we didn't fly home. I know I didn't swim home, and I didn't hitch hike. The only thing I can think of is we probably came by train.

Daughter What was it like when you got home?

Dad   Oh, everything was so different. I couldn't buy a new car. Things were rationed.

Daughter   How long did rationing last after the war?

Dad   Ask your mother[6] because I don't know. She knows all about that. The only thing I ever saw was that Grandpop had stamps to get his tractor gas. I remember seeing his stamps. I think I remember seeing the stamps out for sugar.

Daughter   How were you emotionally?

Dad   When I came home, I was sort of a nervous wreck. I used to wake up under the bed at home. I'd wake up and wonder why I'm under the bed. This was quite often. I'd get mad at myself. One night, my mother decided she was going to look into this. She heard the mail plane going over, so she came into my room, and I crawled out of bed to go underneath the bed. I thought it was the Betty Bomber. She grabbed my wrist and pulled me out. That was the last time I went under the bed. I thought we were being bombed, and I was so used to getting down in a hole like the ones we had dug. We had palm trees and sand bags over it, and that's where I had gone on the islands for shelter.

Daughter   How were you physically? You said your hair grew back after the radiation from the atomic bomb had caused it to fall out. Did you ever have any kind of lasting illness from having been in the Pacific?

Dad   I did get malaria. They gave us these Atabrine tablets. Don't ask me to spell it. You put them in your canteen. You drank that. It was supposed to prevent malaria, but I got a little malaria. My finger nails turned yellow. I had one attack where I perspired. Then, after a while I was just freezing. I went to a doctor, and he said, "You will never get over this; you will have this the rest of your life." He gave me some pills. I decided I was not gonna take the pills the rest of my life. I stopped taking them, and I never got a malaria attack again.

Daughter   Wow, that's great!

Dad   Eugene Nelson, who had been on our ball team, was in New Guinea during WWII. He got malaria, and he never got over it. We dated twin girls one time. We were going to go dancing; but he scared the girls. First, he was shivering, and I'm driving. Then he started taking clothes off; oh, he was just perspiring like crazy. That was malaria. He never got over it.

Daughter   So, you were discharged, and at home. Then what?

Dad   I went to Bliss Engineering School in Washington, D.C. I met your mother in August of 1946, and we got married in June of 1947. We had met when I went to work at Sears repairing radios. She worked in the office. Later, I started working at RCA. In about 1950, our neighbor told me they needed a communications officer in the National Guard. He said, "I understand that you went through Radio School. We need a communications officer in the National Guard real bad."

Daughter So that started your military involvement after WWII? You came home a sergeant first class, but you retired as a major. How did that come about?

Dad School, a lot of school. I had to take all these classes and tests.

Daughter What ranks did you have in between?

Dad It goes private, corporal, buck sergeant, sergeant first class, master sergeant, second lieutenant, then first lieutenant, then captain, then major.

Anyway, I took all the tests, and I had to go to OCS (Officer Candidate School.) I did it through the tests, and I really passed them. Finally, I got an order saying I was a second lieutenant. I started teaching for Uncle Sam in both the Army and the Navy. They even sent me to Germany to teach. That's where we were with the Russians across the river, and our guns pointed at each other. At night time, they did their dances on the bridge, and they'd swap fur caps for American watches. The next morning, the guns were still pointed at each other.

Daughter   A lot of veterans when they came home didn't want to talk about the war. Was that true for you also?

Dad   As a crew, we decided we didn't want to talk about it. We saw too much, but then, maybe, let's say after 20 years, I would have liked to talk to Baldasti. I wanted to say, "Are you still passing out when you see the needle coming for a shot?" They're gone, though, you know.

Daughter   So, you never saw any of them again after the war?

Dad   Never. Well, actually, your mother and I went to a reunion out in Texas maybe 30 years later for anybody that belonged to the Seventh Air Force, 47th Squadron.

Daughter   Wasn't it the Army Air Corp? Didn't the Air Force only come later?

Dad   That came later. In fact, I think it changed the name a year after I got out, maybe in '47. I think they called it Air Force in '47. But throughout the war, it was the Army Air Corps. We even had missions for the Navy when we dropped torpedoes. I mean the Navy gave us those missions even though we were called Army Air Corps. They told us what ships they wanted us to attack. In '47, the Air Force became a separate entity.

Daughter So, then you had a reunion, and you ran into some of your crew?

Dad Not my crew, but one guy I had remembered from the squadron.

Daughter You had seen the cloud. Was that something you told people or not?

Dad I never talked about the cloud. Nope. Not even at RCA; I had good friends at RCA, and I never talked about it. I don't even think I told my family.

Daughter Not until we were teenagers. You started to tell us some stories, then. You are, I suspect, the last living American to have seen the cloud. During the war, you know, you were sort of like a select group that witnessed an incredible event.

Dad There was the guy I met swimming at the rec center who had flown by the cloud on the other side, but yeah, he passed away a couple years ago. Who knows how many planes were returning that day to Okinawa. I don't know; I will never know. I have no idea. It might have been just two. It might have been fifty. Who knows, you know. I was amazed when I talked with this guy that he said, "You mean you saw the cloud?" I said, "Yeah." He said, "Where were —?" I said, "I saw it on my right". "Oh", he said, "I saw it on my left." We must have been only miles apart, you know.

Daughter   One final question, is there anything you would like to say to future generations?

Dad   Yeah. Nobody really "wins" in a war. The losses are terrible on both sides. I wish leaders who are considering a war would go to a battlefield and look at the thousands of grave markers and realize the terrible cost of war. You lose thousands of people, mostly young people, and their families lose sons and daughters.

Daughter   Dad, thank you for sharing your story. You had amazing experiences and like every person who serves his or her country in the military, your story needs to be told.

Notes

1   KP stands for Kitchen Police. A soldier is sometimes "put on KP" as punishment for a minor infraction committed while in uniform. Duties often included washing dishes and food preparation such as peeling potatoes.

2   Tokyo Rose was the nickname given by Allied troops in the South Pacific during World War II to all female English-speaking radio broadcasters of Japanese propaganda, The programs were broadcast in the South Pacific and North America to demoralize Allied troops and their families at home by emphasizing troops' wartime difficulties and military losses. Most soldiers said they recognized that the information was propaganda, but they liked hearing the American music that was played.

3 Sea Bees was the nickname for the United States Naval Construction Battalions. The name came from the initials "C.B." for Construction Battalion.

4 Zero was a name given to a fighter airplane with a single seat used effectively by the Japanese during WWII.

5 Emperor Hirohito made a recording announcing the surrender of Japan which was broadcast in Japan. It was translated into English and the translation was broadcast to Allied forces.

6 Carmen (Charlie's wife, Connie's mother) said, "You had to have them for shoes; one pair a year. You had to have them for canned goods and a lot of other things. I think you had to have them for meat, and one thing I particularly remember is that if you wanted to buy a tube of toothpaste, you had to turn in an empty tube.

ACKNOWLEDGEMENTS

- Chris Hostetter – for transcribing the interview
- James Reddig – for recording the interview
- Matthew Lee Patek – for cover design and all photographic work
- Darlene Graham – for editing and proofreading
- Cathy Gust – for proofreading
- Vicki Reddig Maassen – for editing
  Kim Wittel – for advising on publishing
- Carmen and Dale Bezzard –for proofreading
- John Kirby – for advising
- Elaine Normile (Vinoy Hotel historian) – for supplying a photo

Our deepest gratitude to Adam Robinson, who brought everything together in record time.

ABOUT THE CO-AUTHORS

DR. DENNIS DENENBERG is a nationally known speaker about REAL heroes and their importance to kids and adults. Visit HEROES4US.COM, to read about his work and to order a copy of *50 American Heroes Every Kid Should Meet*. He continues his work on heroes by writing a monthly column (called "Dr. D's Mystery Hero") for *Cobblestone*, a children's history magazine.

A Phi Beta Kappa graduate of The College of William and Mary, he obtained his doctorate from the Pennsylvania State University. During his 30 years as an educator, Dr. D was a high school history teacher, an elementary principal, and assistant superintendent of schools, and finally a Professor at Millersville University.

In addition to promoting REAL heroes, Dr. D loves to garden. Residing in Lancaster, PA, he opens his full acre of gardens and themed home (Wizard of Oz and art deco) to any charity at no charge for fund-raising.

His personal heroes include his Mom and Dad, his speech teachers (he had a severe speech problem as a child), his 8th grade history teacher (Mr. Hildebrand), his sister, Diana, who battled breast cancer for 18 courageous years, and of course, Major Charlie Reddig!

CONNIE REDDIG KIRBY, along with her sister Vicki, and brother Jim, grew up hearing their father's favorite stories (mostly the ones about head-hunters, airplanes, and a mischievous pygmy monkey.) As adults they heard his more somber stories about WWII, and they asked their father repeatedly to write down these memories. Their mother Carmen has written down many memories from her life, but their father has always enjoyed talking more than writing. After the death of Connie's brother Jim, his son James offered to record his grandfather telling some of his stories and the idea for a book was born.

Connie graduated from Millersville University in 1974 with degrees in biology and general science and received her master's degree in gifted education from the same university in 1981.

She taught 7th grade science at Ephrata Middle School, Ephrata, PA, from 1974-2009. She had grown up and attended schools in the same school district and now serves as a board member for the Ephrata Area Education Foundation.

She also serves as co-chair of the Christian Education Committee, develops the Sunday School curriculum, and teaches Sunday School at Salem Lutheran Church in Ephrata.

Connie and husband John, a retired university biology professor, reside in Lititz, PA.

Charles and Carmen Reddig, a current photo

Made in the USA
Middletown, DE
23 July 2018